Little RIDDLERS

Derbyshire & Nottinghamshire Poets

Edited By Megan Roberts

First published in Great Britain in 2018 by:

YoungWriters

Young Writers
Remus House
Coltsfoot Drive
Peterborough
PE2 9BF
Telephone: 01733 890066
Website: www.youngwriters.co.uk

FOREWORD

Dear Reader,

Are you ready to get your thinking caps on to puzzle your way through this wonderful collection?

Young Writers' Little Riddlers competition set out to encourage young writers to create their own riddles. Their answers could be whatever or whoever their imaginations desired; from people to places, animals to objects, food to seasons. Riddles are a great way to further the children's use of poetic expression, including onomatopoeia and similes, as well as encourage them to 'think outside the box' by providing clues without giving the answer away immediately.

All of us here at Young Writers believe in the importance of inspiring young children to produce creative writing, including poetry, and we feel that seeing their own riddles in print will keep that creative spirit burning brightly and proudly.
We hope you enjoy riddling your way through this book as much as we enjoyed reading all the entries.

CONTENTS

Jack Mark Baker (5)	54
Imogen Goodwin (5)	55
Louie Lambert-Coates (4)	56

Heathfield Primary School, Basford

Connie James (7)	57
Lacey Jo Radage-Claven (6)	58
Taylor Rain Connolly (7)	59
Troy Shepherd (7)	60
Vismaya Kannan (7)	61
Jacob Bolger-Gregory (7)	62
Dexter Peacock (6)	63
Nada El-Shakmak (7)	64
Victoria Hyde (7)	65
Riley Yeadon-Barratt (7)	66
Emilia Sitima (7)	67
Jaya Kaur (7)	68
Zunairah Mahmood (7)	69
Maxwell Haywood (7)	70
Rory Sneath (6)	71

Langley Mill CE (C) Infant & Nursery School, Langley Mill

Mia Grace Cooper (7)	72
Ronan Haslam (7)	73
Kaja Bagniewska (6)	74
Avie-May Pouncett (7)	75
Alfie Carr (6)	76
Oscar Lee Urry (7)	77
Katie Janet Rose Goulding (6)	78
Tommie Ben Brigett (6)	79
Tyler Chaplin (7)	80
Daisy Louise Hutsby (7)	81
Rufus Raynor (7)	82
Piper Brown (7)	83
Hayley Guilar-Linton (7)	84
Rosalie Harbon (7)	85
Angel Ebony Nixon (7)	86
Katelyn Tatham (6)	87
Aaron Swan (7)	88
Ryan Everest (7)	89

Gage Lower (7)	90
Cole Verney (6)	91
Georgina Louise Bull (7)	92
Kayleigh May Hallam (7)	93

Leverton CE Academy, North Leverton

Jacob Goodwin (6)	94
Eliza Florence Sirrell (6)	95
Tiarna Jane Bentley-Cresswell (7)	96
Ruby Mai Gardiner (6)	97
Megan Oates (6)	98
Isabelle McCreight (7)	99
Jake Turner (6)	100
Lukas O'Donnell (6)	101
Aidan J Hennessy (6)	102
Connor Griffin (7)	103
Casey Sullivan (6)	104
Simon Malek (7)	105
Charlie John Phillips (6)	106
Callum Brady-Gould (7)	107

Meadow Farm Community Primary School, Chaddesden

Kevin Vu (6)	108
Theo Fernyhough-Tye (6)	109
Lottie Rose Kelk (5)	110

Newstead Primary School, Newstead Village

Grace Lauren Roseanna Gilchrist (6)	111
Lois Giles (7)	112
Anabelle Charlotte McDonnell (7)	113
Jessica Powner (7)	114
Aimee Tomlinson (7)	115
Daisy Kieran (7)	116
Charlie Bennett (6)	117
Isaac Cooling (6)	118
Emma Marie Raynor (7)	119

Jasper Atkin (6)	120
Brooke Summerton (6)	121
Mia-Bella Lynn Astill (7)	122
Max Howarth (6)	123
Farron Leverton-Jones (7)	124
Lilly-Mae Warsop (7)	125
Suzie-May Smith (6)	126
Maegen Smith (7)	127
Klara Young (6)	128

St Oswald's CE Primary School, Ashbourne

Henry Hathaway (7)	129
Lily Jennings (7)	130
Harry Marsh (6)	131
Nancy Lou Archer (6)	132
Ray Marsh (7)	133
William Davies (6)	134
Sadie Burton (7)	135
Lenny Lourie (7)	136
Luciana Checketts (7)	137
Ottilie Godden (7)	138
Zoe-Dee Barclay (7)	139
Poppy Clayton (7)	140
Lily Butt (7)	141
Myles Edward Davies (7)	142
Taylor Hambleton-Harrison (6)	143
Oliver Whitaker (6)	144

Whaley Bridge Primary School, Whaley Bridge

Cairistiona Smith (7)	145
Kit Garside (5)	146
Nate Cooper (7)	147
Darcy Hodgson (6)	148
Nancy Caitlin Kerr (7)	149
Grace Vickers (6)	150
Sophie Ashworth (6)	151
Frankie Margaret Dorothy Yaya Knowles (7)	152
Hollie Jones (6)	153
Sebastian Hilditch (7)	154

THE POEMS

Running And Climbing

I like to run around
And I make a squeaky sound,
In the day, you won't catch the sight of me,
In the night, I might just bite.
I live in a cage
And my colour is beige.
What am I?

Answer: A hamster.

Alinah-Lillie Isabelle Whitaker (5)
Albany Infant & Nursery School, Stapleford

Elliott's Secret Animal

I have venom,
I lay eggs,
I am semiaquatic.
I live in Australia and Tasmania,
I have a duck bill, a beaver tail and otter feet,
I am on the back of an Australian coin,
What am I?

Answer: A platypus.

Elliott Jack Kane (7)
Albany Infant & Nursery School, Stapleford

Mysterious

I may look a little odd,
I have a green bod,
I have three eyes
And I live in the skies.
I have friends who are yellow and blue,
I have a ship, but not for you.
What am I?

Answer: An alien.

Arlo James Wallis (6)
Albany Infant & Nursery School, Stapleford

I Dig A Lot And Think A Lot And I Eat Leaves

I eat leaves,
I have big, bushy ears.
I sleep up to eighteen hours a day,
I have a pouch when my baby is born.
I have grey fur,
I have sharp claws.
What am I?

Answer: A koala bear.

Sophia Chapman (7)

Albany Infant & Nursery School, Stapleford

A Prickly Friend

I live in the woods
And I eat crunchy bugs.
I go out at night
And go to bed when it's light.
I am spiky and round
But I don't make a sound.
What am I?

Answer: A hedgehog.

Ethan Kenney (6)
Albany Infant & Nursery School, Stapleford

Pegasus

I have a rainbow mane,
I have a spiky horn.
I have huge, sparkly wings to fly with,
I live all around the world.
Wherever I go, rainbows follow.
What am I?

Answer: A unicorn.

Khloe Barnes (7)
Albany Infant & Nursery School, Stapleford

Hard-Working

I have a claw,
I live outside,
I dig holes,
I'm at the side of the road,
I don't have legs,
I'm controlled by a man.
What am I?

Answer: A digger.

Nicholas Hales (7)
Albany Infant & Nursery School, Stapleford

Living In The Antarctic

I like to eat fish.
I am a type of bird
But I can't fly.
I live in the Antarctic.
What am I?

Answer: A penguin.

Jamie-Leigh Jackson (6)
Albany Infant & Nursery School, Stapleford

What Am I?

I graze on lots of scrumptious grass
And I never get bored of it.
Amazingly, I am in the beautiful horse
family.
I have a jet-black mane.
I have beautiful, jet-black and magnificent,
white stripes to camouflage,
So do my friends, so animals can't get us.
What am I?

Answer: A zebra.

Oscar Henry Gascoyne (7)
Asquith Primary School, Mansfield

What Am I?

I'm very small and very cute.
My diet is insects and grubs.
I do everything with my family.
Although we look similar, I am not a
mongoose.
The country I come from is Africa,
In the hot savannah.
One of us looks out while the others play.
What am I?

Answer: A meerkat.

Caitlin Bamford (7)
Asquith Primary School, Mansfield

What Am I?

My teeth are as sharp as razors.
I have four powerful legs so I can run fast.
I have hundreds of black, thin stripes.
I always eat meat because it is my favourite food.
I have orange fur all over my body.
Although we look similar, I am not a zebra.
What am I?

Answer: A tiger.

Brenna Strouther (7)
Asquith Primary School, Mansfield

What Am I?

Although we look similar, I'm not a horse.
I live in amazing Africa.
My stripes are different patterns.
I like grass and twigs.
I live in the heat.
My legs are long so I can run fast.
I have stripes like a tiger but I'm not a cat.
What am I?

Answer: A zebra.

Dylan James Alfie Scrase (7)
Asquith Primary School, Mansfield

What Am I?

I am a really good swimmer.
During the day, I eat lots of fish.
Although we look similar, I am not a panda.
Every day, I need to take care of my babies
and take them to bed.
I am white and I have a furry coat.
I love to be in the snow.
What am I?

Answer: A polar bear.

Faezah Kamali (7)
Asquith Primary School, Mansfield

What Am I?

I eat juicy fruit.
I have short ears and little eyes.
I blend into the rocks so people can't see me.
I have short legs.
My leathery skin keeps me safe from things that try to bite me.
I have two horns that are very strong.
What am I?

Answer: A rhinoceros.

Lucy Frances Sheppard (7)
Asquith Primary School, Mansfield

What Am I?

My body has thick fur like a tiger.
There are many black spots on my body
So I can camouflage in the light brown
grass.
I run faster than people
And I have four strong legs.
When I cry, I leave black lines across my
face.
What am I?

Answer: A cheetah.

Kai Green (7)

Asquith Primary School, Mansfield

What Am I?

Although I am greedy, I am not a lion.
My group lives in the massive savannah of
Africa.
I eat similar animals to lions.
I've got sharp claws and sharp teeth.
I've got a large mouth.
My babies are called cubs.
What am I?

Answer: A tiger.

Dominik Lubasinski (7)
Asquith Primary School, Mansfield

What Am I?

I only have two tall legs.
I eat fish.
I don't run fast because I'm clumsy.
Although we look similar, I'm not an ostrich.
Surprisingly, I like to balance on one leg.
I have beautiful, pink feathers.
What am I?

Answer: A flamingo.

Dakota Storm Wickham (7)

Asquith Primary School, Mansfield

What Am I?

Every day, I look after my babies and I get them food.
I may bite.
Some of us are in zoos.
In the wild, I have lots of food.
I have black and white fur and I can climb.
My babies can climb.
What am I?

Answer: A lemur.

Amy Collins (7)
Asquith Primary School, Mansfield

Clever Animals

I fight enemies for my family.
My body is tough and strong.
Surprisingly, I have huge feet.
My tusks are long and pointy.
I'm not a rhino.
I use my unique trunk to eat and drink.
What am I?

Answer: An elephant.

Catelynn Keogh (7)
Asquith Primary School, Mansfield

What Am I?

I have long whiskers and there are three on each side.
The African savannah is my home.
My teeth are very, very sharp.
My cubs have tiny feet.
I have stripes that stretch out on my back.
What am I?

Answer: A tiger.

Brooke Joyce Kerrison (7)
Asquith Primary School, Mansfield

What Am I?

My legs are long so I can run fast.
Although we look similar, I'm not a donkey.
I eat grass off the ground.
I have stripes like a tiger but I'm not a cat.
I live in a herd.
What am I?

Answer: A zebra.

Kian Hayes (7)
Asquith Primary School, Mansfield

What Am I?

I have very sharp teeth.
My favourite food is a zebra.
I have a very furry tail.
Africa is where I live.
I am the king of the animals.
I have a very large mane.
What am I?

Answer: A lion.

Harley Dee (7)
Asquith Primary School, Mansfield

What Am I?

Although we look similar, I am not a horse
Our legs are strong because we need to run
I live in Africa
My stripes are like a tiger's
I am not a cat
What am I?

Answer: A zebra.

Summer James (7)
Asquith Primary School, Mansfield

What Am I?

I have little ears,
I have sharp claws.
I have pointy teeth,
I have a long tail.
I have long legs to run fast with,
I have four spotty legs.
What am I?

Answer: A cheetah.

Tyler Peter Davies (7)
Asquith Primary School, Mansfield

Animal Puzzle

It lives in the oceans.
It jumps in and out of the ocean.
It eats shellfish.
When it goes out of the water, that means that it's breathing.
Its fins help it to swim.
It has fins to help it go faster.
What animal is it?

Answer: A dolphin.

Blake Higginbotham (6)
Asterdale Primary School, Spondon

Animal Puzzle

It's pink and its beak is yellow.
It lives in the water.
It also has a bit of black on its beak.
It can swim really fast.
It gets lots of fish for dinner.
It drinks a lot of water.
What animal is it?

Answer: A flamingo.

Sohampreet Kour (6)
Asterdale Primary School, Spondon

Animal Puzzle

It eats acorns and nuts.
It flies.
It lives in the jungle.
It copies people.
It lives in a tree.
It is made of feathers.
It has claws to smash stuff.
It is warm-blooded.
What animal is it?

Answer: A parrot.

Sam Jakeway (6)
Asterdale Primary School, Spondon

Animal Puzzle

It is an animal that can swim and jump.
It is white when it is a baby.
It lives in a cold place.
It lives in the ocean.
It has fins and it is furry and it has four fins.
It is grey.
What animal is it?

Answer: A seal.

Lillie-Mai Bruckshaw (6)
Asterdale Primary School, Spondon

Animal Puzzle

It lives in a dark cave.
It has a big fight.
Its belly keeps it warm.
It has a furry tail.
It has fur.
It has brown eyes.
It has little paws.
What animal is it?

Answer: A meerkat.

Freddie Iredale (5)
Asterdale Primary School, Spondon

Animal Puzzle

It eats meat.
It has a black nose.
It lives in a kennel.
It drinks water.
The eyes' colours are black and white.
It has sparkly and shiny teeth.
What animal is it?

Answer: A dog.

Lexi Mai Maddocks (6)
Asterdale Primary School, Spondon

Animal Puzzle

I have a big, trusty tusk.
I have a fish's tail.
I live with icebergs.
I have black marks on my body.
I live in Antarctica.
I live with my friends.
What am I?

Answer: A narwhal.

Jack Flint (6)
Asterdale Primary School, Spondon

Animal Puzzle

It carries its babies with its teeth.
It lives on dry land.
It has sharp claws.
It is vicious.
Its babies are golden.
It hunts for meat.
What animal is it?

Answer: A lion.

Isla Lee (6)
Asterdale Primary School, Spondon

Animal Puzzle

I have claws and I can fly.
I can go in the leaves
And I live in the jungle.
I can talk.
I have feathers.
I am a bird and I am beautiful.
What am I?

Answer: A parrot.

Vana Evelyn Rudkin (5)
Asterdale Primary School, Spondon

Animal Puzzle

It can glow in the dark.
It can sting you.
It lives in the water.
It sleeps on a rock.
It can change.
It has bumpy tentacles.
What animal is it?

Answer: A jellyfish.

Corey Jonathan O'Brien Hinkson (6)
Asterdale Primary School, Spondon

Dangerous Fighter

It can climb.
It can fight.
It has claws.
It eats leftover food like apples.
It has four legs.
It has black stripes on it.
What animal is it?

Answer: A raccoon.

Freddie Watson (6)

Asterdale Primary School, Spondon

Animal Puzzle

It has long whiskers.
It eats meat.
Its body is covered in fur.
It lives in my house.
It has four legs.
It has a long tail.
What animal is it?

Answer: A cat.

Lillie Doherty (6)
Asterdale Primary School, Spondon

Animal Puzzle

It has sharp toes.
It has a tail.
It eats meat.
It can bite.
It has four feet.
It lived thousands of years ago.
What animal is it?

Answer: A dinosaur.

Louie-James David Tivey (6)

Asterdale Primary School, Spondon

Animal Puzzle

It has two feet.
It has two eyes.
It is little but not forever.
It is cute.
It eats seeds.
It has yellow feathers.
What animal is it?

Answer: A chick.

Noah Robin Simms McCabe (6)
Asterdale Primary School, Spondon

Animal Puzzle

It has a black mane.
It has a black tail.
It has hooves.
It has four legs.
It is furry.
It can run fast.
What animal is it?

Answer: A horse.

Morgan Davis (6)
Asterdale Primary School, Spondon

Animal Puzzle

It can run fast.
It has a black tail.
It has fur.
It has white fur.
It eats meat.
It has a soft nose.
What animal is it?

Answer: A cat.

Lacey Richards (6)
Asterdale Primary School, Spondon

Animal Puzzle

It has some sharp teeth.
It has black eyes.
It has fluff when it goes to bed.
It has ears.
What animal is it?

Answer: A hamster.

Ava Lucy Bednall (5)

Asterdale Primary School, Spondon

Animal Puzzle

It is big.
It runs slowly.
It has sharp claws.
It has two legs.
What animal is it?

Answer: A dinosaur.

Lucas Hollingworth (6)
Asterdale Primary School, Spondon

Super Wet

I am wet, I am cold
And I come out of nowhere.
There are millions of us.
People don't like it when I come,
But I am needed.
What am I?

Answer: Rain.

Kyron Harding (7)
Burford Primary & Nursery School, Arnold

What Am I?

I have a long nose.
I have four legs.
I have a tail like a brush.
I have spikes on my tongue.
My baby rests on my back.
I spend a lot of time by myself.
I eat 30,000 ants every day.
What am I?

Answer: An anteater.

Flora Alice Clowes (5)
Clifton CE Primary School, Clifton

The Flyer

I am thin and scrawny.
I am as pretty as a lady.
I drink pollen from a flower.
I am shorter and smaller than a gorilla.
I am graceful and beautiful.
I used to be a caterpillar.
What am I?

Answer: A butterfly.

Katy Sellers (6)
Clifton CE Primary School, Clifton

The Sleepy Baby

I sleep for a long time at night.
I walk very slowly.
I live in hollow trees.
I eat insects and fruit and leaves.
I am as small as a monkey.
I cry and shriek like a baby.
What am I?

Answer: A bush baby.

Adelaide Ratcliffe (5)
Clifton CE Primary School, Clifton

The Grass Eater

I have a big tummy to roll around with.
I love to eat grass.
I have big feet.
I have short teeth.
I have big eyes.
I love to roll in the mud.
What am I?

Answer: A hippopotamus.

Isaac Hagan (6)
Clifton CE Primary School, Clifton

Light Head

I have a light on my head.
I have a blue body.
I love meat.
I would love to meet you because you're meat.
I am as scary as a monster.
What am I?

Answer: An anglerfish.

Lyla Griffiths (6)
Clifton CE Primary School, Clifton

What Am I?

I have pretty hair.
I have a fat tummy.
I have lots of hair.
I am free.
I eat bananas.
What am I?

Answer: A chimpanzee.

Scarlett Moon (4)

Clifton CE Primary School, Clifton

The Meat Eater

I have black spots.
I eat meat.
I am yellow.
I have sharp claws.
I like to chase zebras.
What am I?

Answer: A leopard.

Harry Hickinson (6)
Clifton CE Primary School, Clifton

Sleepy Sid

I have grey fur.
I hang on a tree.
I sleep on a branch.
I eat leaves.
I walk slowly.
What am I?

Answer: A sloth.

Ruby Jac Lemon (5)
Clifton CE Primary School, Clifton

Snappy

I have sharp teeth.
I have colourful scales.
I have a red tail.
I eat fish and meat.
What am I?

Answer: A piranha.

Archie David Meadows (4)
Clifton CE Primary School, Clifton

The Slow Hanger

I hang in trees.
I eat many leaves.
I eat sticks from the floor.
I am very slow.
What am I?

Answer: A sloth.

Lachlan Alexander Fielding (5)

Clifton CE Primary School, Clifton

The Fly Eater

I live everywhere.
I eat flies.
I am as scary as a ghost.
I spin webs.
What am I?

Answer: A spider.

Jack Mark Baker (5)
Clifton CE Primary School, Clifton

The Spotty Mystery

I purr.
I am scary.
I eat deer.
I sleep in a forest.
What am I?

Answer: A jaguar.

Imogen Goodwin (5)
Clifton CE Primary School, Clifton

Softy

I am stripy,
I have furry ears,
I have four legs,
What am I?

Answer: A Bengal tiger.

Louie Lambert-Coates (4)
Clifton CE Primary School, Clifton

Cutest Animal

I am normally white but sometimes I'm pink.
I always have four legs.
I am a herbivore.
I am very cute.
Did you know that I'm very sparkly?
I am very fast.
What am I?

Answer: A unicorn.

Connie James (7)
Heathfield Primary School, Basford

My Riddle

I am very pretty.
I can be lots of colours.
Lots of people smell me.
Some people grow me.
Some people give me to the people they love.
I sometimes grow in grass.
What am I?

Answer: A flower.

Lacey Jo Radage-Claven (6)
Heathfield Primary School, Basford

Cutest

I am an animal.
I have four legs.
I have whiskers.
I am cute.
I eat chicken.
I purr.
I have lots of spots.
I am an omnivore.
I am very fast.
What am I?

Answer: A kitten.

Taylor Rain Connolly (7)
Heathfield Primary School, Basford

Guess What I Am

I walk on two legs.
I would be a giant to you.
I'm a carnivore.
I've got a loud roar.
I can run as fast as a cheetah.
I'm extinct.
What am I?

Answer: A carcharodontosaurus.

Troy Shepherd (7)
Heathfield Primary School, Basford

I Am Real, Not Magical

I have a horn.
I live under the sea.
I am a sort of whale.
I am really not magical.
Most people think I am magical.
I am linked to unicorns.
What am I?

Answer: A narwhal.

Vismaya Kannan (7)
Heathfield Primary School, Basford

What Am I?

I am a dinosaur.
I am big.
I have a long neck.
I have a tiny tail.
I have a lump on my head.
My name begins with a 'B'.
What am I?

Answer: A brachiosaurus.

Jacob Bolger-Gregory (7)
Heathfield Primary School, Basford

Superhero!

I go out in the night.
I am very mad.
I have three sharp claws.
I am crazy.
I am savage.
I howl.
I sleep in the morning.
Who am I?

Answer: Wolverine.

Dexter Peacock (6)

Heathfield Primary School, Basford

Long, Long, Long

I am an insect.
I am long.
I have sixteen legs.
I have antennae.
I sleep in a cocoon.
My mum is a butterfly.
What am I?

Answer: A caterpillar.

Nada El-Shakmak (7)
Heathfield Primary School, Basford

Stripy, Stripy, Stripy!

I am white.
I have a long tail.
I am a carnivore.
I have sharp claws.
I have sharp teeth.
I have stripes.
What am I?

Answer: A white tiger.

Victoria Hyde (7)
Heathfield Primary School, Basford

A Season

I am cold.
I am cold in January, February and
December.
I am between Spring and Autumn.
I begin with 'W'.
What am I?

Answer: Winter.

Riley Yeadon-Barratt (7)
Heathfield Primary School, Basford

Speedy, Speedy, Speedy!

I am an animal.
I am brown.
I am a herbivore.
I am very speedy.
I have very long ears.
I can leap.
What am I?

Answer: A hare.

Emilia Sitima (7)
Heathfield Primary School, Basford

My Lovely Pet

I have spots.
I have got sharp teeth.
I have got four legs.
I have got a long tail.
I am fast.
What am I?

Answer: A cheetah.

Jaya Kaur (7)
Heathfield Primary School, Basford

Try And Guess What I Am

I am an animal,
I can live in a zoo,
I am a type of bird,
I am pink,
I stand on one leg,
What am I?

Answer: A flamingo.

Zunairah Mahmood (7)
Heathfield Primary School, Basford

What Am I?

I am like a human.
I can open boxes.
I like to swing on trees.
I am furry.
I like bananas.
What am I?

Answer: A monkey.

Maxwell Haywood (7)
Heathfield Primary School, Basford

What Am I?

I have lots of spots.
I have a fluffy tail.
I am yellow.
I am speedy.
What am I?

Answer: A cheetah.

Rory Sneath (6)
Heathfield Primary School, Basford

Guess My Minibeast

I like the sun but I don't like the rain.
I look like petals.
Sometimes, I land on flowers.
Sometimes, I camouflage.
I fly in the sky.
I lay my eggs on a leaf.
I look like a flying bow.
I like being in a group.
I like flowers.
I like the petals of flowers.
I like to play.
What am I?

Answer: A butterfly.

Mia Grace Cooper (7)

Langley Mill CE (C) Infant & Nursery School,
Langley Mill

Insect Riddle

I can fly up in the sky.
I look like a crane fly.
I live in the wild.
On my face, I have two eyes.
I don't camouflage.
I am found in hot places.
I have four scary, black legs.
My babies are first laid in eggs.
I am as little as a crane fly.
I have grippers on my legs.
What am I?

Answer: A mosquito.

Ronan Haslam (7)

Langley Mill CE (C) Infant & Nursery School,
Langley Mill

Minibeast Mystery

I feel like a bundle of hair
My favourite place is in the dark
Gardens and deserts are my home
Sometimes I am grey
Sometimes I am black
People are sometimes scared of me
I have eight legs
On my head, you will only see six eyes
What am I?

Answer: A spider.

Kaja Bagniewska (6)

Langley Mill CE (C) Infant & Nursery School,
Langley Mill

Guess What I Am

I live in South America.
Birds are my favourite treat.
I like the shade and places that creak.
I don't like the rain.
I am scary and hairy.
My fangs are poisonous.
I like to crawl on eight legs.
What am I?

Answer: A Goliath bird-eating spider.

Avie-May Pouncett (7)

Langley Mill CE (C) Infant & Nursery School,
Langley Mill

What Am I?

I blend in with the green grass
When I'm about seven months old, I start to grow
My home is a bush
I don't live in a group
I eat juicy leaves
When I am born, I am very small
I have two eyes on my big head
What am I?

Answer: A greenfly.

Alfie Carr (6)
Langley Mill CE (C) Infant & Nursery School,
Langley Mill

Guess The Minibeast

I eat green flies.
I squirt yellow liquid when I'm scared.
I have six fat legs.
You can find me on leaves.
I like to bathe in the sun
And sometimes I like the shade.
I can fly in the sky.
What am I?

Answer: A ladybird.

Oscar Lee Urry (7)

Langley Mill CE (C) Infant & Nursery School,
Langley Mill

What Am I?

My favourite food is juicy, green flies.
I like hiding in people's bedrooms and under their beds.
I have eight very hairy legs.
I make webs in trees to catch yummy flies.
Watch out, I might bite you.
What am I?

Answer: A spider.

Katie Janet Rose Goulding (6)
Langley Mill CE (C) Infant & Nursery School,
Langley Mill

What Am I?

My favourite place to hide is under logs and rocks.
I live in the trees.
I have eight fat legs.
I crawl everywhere.
I make cobwebs everywhere.
I eat juicy, green flies.
I am black and dark.
What am I?

Answer: A spider.

Tommie Ben Brigett (6)

Langley Mill CE (C) Infant & Nursery School, Langley Mill

Guess The Minibeast

I hide under logs and rocks.
My fangs are long and sharp.
I am sometimes scary.
I have eight black eyes.
You might see me crawling downstairs.
I can be small or big.
I am hairy and black.
What am I?

Answer: A spider.

Tyler Chaplin (7)

Langley Mill CE (C) Infant & Nursery School,
Langley Mill

A Minibeast Riddle

My home is in the sky.
Nectar is my favourite treat.
I have long, fragile antennae.
I can't fly in the rain.
Honey is something I am good at making.
My colours are yellow and black.
What am I?

Answer: A bee.

Daisy Louise Hutsby (7)
Langley Mill CE (C) Infant & Nursery School,
Langley Mill

Guess What I Am

I am black and hairy.
Some people think I'm scary.
You might find me eating a juicy fly.
I love places that are dark and high.
I sometimes have two eyes.
Damp places are great.
What am I?

Answer: A spider.

Rufus Raynor (7)

Langley Mill CE (C) Infant & Nursery School,
Langley Mill

Minibeast Mystery

I feel tickly on your hand.
I am very, very small.
You can find me under logs in the woods.
My colour is grey.
I have antennae.
I have no eyes.
I live in the ground.
What am I?

Answer: A woodlouse.

Piper Brown (7)
Langley Mill CE (C) Infant & Nursery School,
Langley Mill

Guess The Minibeast

You might find me in the sky.
I am yellow and black.
I live in a hive.
My wings are transparent.
If you touch me, I might sting you.
I have five eyes.
I eat pollen.
What am I?

Answer: A bee.

Hayley Guilar-Linton (7)
Langley Mill CE (C) Infant & Nursery School,
Langley Mill

What Am I?

My favourite food is pollen.
I have patterns on my wings.
I am beautiful.
My eyes are scary.
I have big wings.
I am colourful.
I look like a bright flower.
What am I?

Answer: A butterfly.

Rosalie Harbon (7)

Langley Mill CE (C) Infant & Nursery School,
Langley Mill

Guess The Minibeast

I am stripy.
I can't fly in the rain.
I have five eyes.
I live in a hive.
I fly up in the sky.
I am black and yellow.
I make honey.
I have four wings.
What am I?

Answer: A bee.

Angel Ebony Nixon (7)
Langley Mill CE (C) Infant & Nursery School,
Langley Mill

Guess The Minibeast

It has colourful, bright wings.
It is going to catch me.
It has lovely wings.
It has lovely patterns.
It has pretty colours on it.
People step on its body.
What is it?

Answer: A butterfly.

Katelyn Tatham (6)

Langley Mill CE (C) Infant & Nursery School,
Langley Mill

Guess The Creature

I live in the roasting desert.
I eat mostly flies.
I make tapping noises when I run.
I like to bury myself in sand and dark places.
I have eight beady eyes.
What am I?

Answer: A sun spider.

Aaron Swan (7)
Langley Mill CE (C) Infant & Nursery School,
Langley Mill

What Am I?

I crawl on land.
I float on water.
If you come near me, I will bite you.
I am the size of your hand.
I am the biggest spider you've ever seen.
What am I?

Answer: A tarantula.

Ryan Everest (7)

Langley Mill CE (C) Infant & Nursery School,
Langley Mill

Guess The Minibeast

I have a long, soft tail.
I have blue eyes.
I have claws.
I have very sharp teeth.
I am fluffy.
I don't like being wet.
What am I?

Answer: A cat.

Gage Lower (7)
Langley Mill CE (C) Infant & Nursery School,
Langley Mill

Minibeast

I have two eyes in my head.
I am black.
I have a pincer.
I like dark spaces.
You might find me eating a spider.
What am I?

Answer: A scorpion.

Cole Verney (6)

Langley Mill CE (C) Infant & Nursery School,
Langley Mill

Minibeast Riddle

My wings have patterns on.
I have antennae.
I eat pollen.
My eyes are tiny.
You can catch me.
What am I?

Answer: A butterfly.

Georgina Louise Bull (7)

Langley Mill CE (C) Infant & Nursery School,
Langley Mill

What Am I?

I have wings.
I like to eat juicy leaves.
I like to fly.
I have eyes.
What am I?

Answer: A butterfly.

Kayleigh May Hallam (7)
Langley Mill CE (C) Infant & Nursery School,
Langley Mill

A Place To Go

I can give you supreme facts.
I can teach you how to be an acrobat.
I can have a title about a black, crazy bat.
I can give you cool pictures on my pages.
I can be sold in a shop.
I can have information about a map.
What am I?

Answer: A book.

Jacob Goodwin (6)
Leverton CE Academy, North Leverton

What Am I?

I'm as long as a person.
I'm as cute as a horse.
I'm coming to jump on you so watch out!
I'm as fluffy as a tiger.
I can fall asleep on you.
I can make you tired too.
What am I?

Answer: A sausage dog.

Eliza Florence Sirrell (6)
Leverton CE Academy, North Leverton

Fluffy

I drink white, gleaming milk.
I am as furry as a lion's mane.
I chase black mice.
I have funny ears like a dog's.
I have beautiful bows in my hair.
I eat smelly fish.
What am I?

Answer: A cat.

Tiarna Jane Bentley-Cresswell (7)
Leverton CE Academy, North Leverton

Furry Ball

I love to sleep and be cosy.
I like to be stroked softly.
I can scratch with my sharp claws.
I have whiskers and paws.
I like to eat mice.
I will purr when I am happy.
What am I?

Answer: A cat.

Ruby Mai Gardiner (6)
Leverton CE Academy, North Leverton

I Can Travel

I have wheels.
I am in the shape of a rectangle.
I have eleven circles.
I have six squares.
I have special lights.
I have a steering wheel.
I have window wipers.
What am I?

Answer: A bus.

Megan Oates (6)
Leverton CE Academy, North Leverton

Summer

I am pink and blue and purple too
I land on you and flutter too
I have a skeleton on the outside
It is very hard to see
I have wings
I have antennae
What am I?

Answer: A butterfly.

Isabelle McCreight (7)
Leverton CE Academy, North Leverton

Hoppy Animal

I am very hoppy.
I am fluffy and brown.
I steal food from a garden.
I am very cheeky.
I love carrots and radishes.
I have a blue, furry coat.
Who am I?

Answer: Peter Rabbit.

Jake Turner (6)
Leverton CE Academy, North Leverton

A Black Creature

I have big, black eyes.
I have a white mohawk on my head.
I am bad.
I wreck the world.
I have a chainsaw in my hand.
I have some claws.
What am I?

Answer: A gremlin.

Lukas O'Donnell (6)
Leverton CE Academy, North Leverton

Flesh Hunting

I eat meat and flesh.
I have razor-sharp teeth.
I have a red belly.
I live in warm rivers.
I hunt in groups.
I can crush bones.
What am I?

Answer: A piranha.

Aidan J Hennessy (6)
Leverton CE Academy, North Leverton

Terrific Transportation

I can be any colour.
I can puff steam out of my funnel.
My wheels are noisy.
I go *choo, choo*.
I take you to a station.
What am I?

Answer: A train.

Connor Griffin (7)
Leverton CE Academy, North Leverton

Frosty

I am cold.
I melt in the sun.
I have sticks for hands.
I have stones for eyes.
I am white.
I have snow for my body.
What am I?

Answer: A snowman.

Casey Sullivan (6)
Leverton CE Academy, North Leverton

A Cold Day

I fall very slowly.
I am not nice outside.
I make it snowy outside.
I am very cold.
I am very fun.
I melt in the sun.
What am I?

Answer: Winter.

Simon Malek (7)
Leverton CE Academy, North Leverton

In The Sea

I can sting fish.
I can sting people.
I live in the sea.
I am long and thin.
I use electricity to attack.
What am I?

Answer: An electric eel.

Charlie John Phillips (6)
Leverton CE Academy, North Leverton

I Bite

I go underwater.
I kill fish.
I kill squid.
I like turtles.
I have a sharp fin.
I have black fins.
What am I?

Answer: A shark.

Callum Brady-Gould (7)
Leverton CE Academy, North Leverton

Thump! Thump! Thump!

I live in the deep, dark sea.
I have huge, sharp teeth.
I eat anything in the sea.
I have a tool on my head.
I am big and sneaky.
I am the king of the sea.
What am I?

Answer: A hammerhead shark.

Kevin Vu (6)

Meadow Farm Community Primary School,
Chaddesden

Jaws

My new teeth never stop growing.
I'm half white and half blue.
I'm a predator.
I can roll my eyes.
Fish are afraid of my sharp smile.
What am I?

Answer: A great white shark.

Theo Fernyhough-Tye (6)
Meadow Farm Community Primary School,
Chaddesden

Honey House

I have stripes.
I have six legs and four wings.
I travel in a swarm.
I have a queen.
I am yellow.
I make honey.
What am I?

Answer: A bee.

Lottie Rose Kelk (5)
Meadow Farm Community Primary School,
Chaddesden

Who Am I?

I am brave.
Once, I killed a bad man.
I am quiet.
My mum was killed in her house,
My mum was alive until then.
I was a baby when that happened,
I was about two.
But now I'm with my cousin,
He gets everything.
It's just not fair
But it's not all bad
Because my cousin fell into a snake cage.
Who am I?

Answer: Harry Potter.

Grace Lauren Roseanna Gilchrist (6)
Newstead Primary School, Newstead Village

Hop, Hop, Hop, Hop!

I am furry.
I don't show my skin.
I am the smallest mammal.
I am not a reptile.
I have long ears.
I don't have floppy ears.
I have pointy whiskers.
I love long carrots.
I am so cute.
What am I?

Answer: A rabbit.

Lois Giles (7)
Newstead Primary School, Newstead Village

Bang, Bang, Boom, Pop

I am loud and sparkly
Glittery but I sound like this:
Crackle, boom, bang, pop!
Kids adore me
And I'm never late for a party or celebration
But I am very colourful.
What am I?

Answer: A firework.

Anabelle Charlotte McDonnell (7)

Newstead Primary School, Newstead Village

Big Or Small?

I get bigger the more you take away.
You can get me in lots of places.
You can make me.
I can be big or small.
Sometimes you can fit in me.
I can be different shapes.
What am I?

Answer: A hole.

Jessica Powner (7)
Newstead Primary School, Newstead Village

The Spook!

I am clear.
I am spooky.
I am here but I'm not.
I might give you a fright
In the middle of the night.
I can move through rooms but I don't need a door.
What am I?

Answer: A ghost.

Aimee Tomlinson (7)
Newstead Primary School, Newstead Village

My Furry Friend!

I am brown.
I am furry.
I can cuddle you
But I can't talk to you.
Some of us are chubby,
Some of us are slim.
What am I?

Answer: A teddy bear.

Daisy Kieran (7)
Newstead Primary School, Newstead Village

Little Black Bandits

I am little.
I carry food to my queen.
I am black.
I have antennae.
I also have six legs.
I am cute but naughty.
What am I?

Answer: An ant.

Charlie Bennett (6)
Newstead Primary School, Newstead Village

In The Wild

I am weird.
I come in different sizes.
I have a curly tail.
I change my colour.
I eat flies.
I have claws.
What am I?

Answer: A chameleon.

Isaac Cooling (6)
Newstead Primary School, Newstead Village

Flappy Wings

I have sharp claws.
I don't have fur
But I have feathers.
My predator is a fox.
I lay your breakfast.
What am I?

Answer: A chicken.

Emma Marie Raynor (7)
Newstead Primary School, Newstead Village

Lava

I am made of huge rocks.
Don't get me mad, I might erupt.
I can be hotter than the sun.
I am huge.
What am I?

Answer: A volcano.

Jasper Atkin (6)
Newstead Primary School, Newstead Village

A Furry Friend

I am furry.
I am cuddly.
I would like to be walked three times a day.
I like chicken.
I like water.
What am I?

Answer: A dog.

Brooke Summerton (6)
Newstead Primary School, Newstead Village

The Gallopers

I am a mammal.
I can gallop
But I can also dance.
I can jump
And you can ride or stroke me.
What am I?

Answer: A horse.

Mia-Bella Lynn Astill (7)
Newstead Primary School, Newstead Village

What Am I?

I am stinky.
I go on your feet.
I like going to the shops
And everywhere else with people.
What am I?

Answer: A stinky sock.

Max Howarth (6)
Newstead Primary School, Newstead Village

Thousands Of Years Ago

I was bigger than a T-rex.
I was camouflaged.
I lived a long time ago.
I lived under the sea.
What am I?

Answer: A dinosaur.

Farron Leverton-Jones (7)
Newstead Primary School, Newstead Village

I Can Gallop

I can gallop, trot and canter
I can take you for a ride
But I am not a car
What am I?

Answer: A horse.

Lilly-Mae Warsop (7)
Newstead Primary School, Newstead Village

Hop

I hop around
I hate water
I love to eat grass, flowers and vegetables
What am I?

Answer: A rabbit.

Suzie-May Smith (6)

Newstead Primary School, Newstead Village

In The Forest

I am black and white,
I come out at night
And I bite your boots.
What am I?

Answer: A badger.

Maegen Smith (7)
Newstead Primary School, Newstead Village

What Am I?

I can swim.
I don't have legs
But I have fins.
What am I?

Answer: A fish.

Klara Young (6)
Newstead Primary School, Newstead Village

Argh!

I run like melted ice cream down a cone on a sunny day.
I'm as red as raspberries and strawberries, ripe and juicy.
I shake the ground like a stone giant running around the earth.
I frighten people when they see me destroying houses, burning like a red-hot bull.
I turn people into statues with my burning hot ash.
I'm as dangerous as a great white shark, don't get in my way.
What am I?

Answer: A volcano.

Henry Hathaway (7)
St Oswald's CE Primary School, Ashbourne

The Amazing Riddle!

They like to run and play,
They do it every day.
They can be short or tall, slim or fat
And they really like to chase everyone's cats.
They love to swim, just like my friend, Tim.
They come in different colours, black, white or brown.
From short to long hair, they really do care.
They are a man's best friend
And stay with you until the end.
What are they?

Answer: Dogs.

Lily Jennings (7)
St Oswald's CE Primary School, Ashbourne

You Can't Find Me

Can you guess what I am?
I come in many different colours,
I come in many different sizes,
Sometimes big and sometimes small.
Sometimes I have a lid,
But sometimes it gets lost.
You can't rub me out
But you can use me in any hand.
You can hold me and you can use me,
You can brighten up a picture with me.
I can get used a lot in schools.
What am I?

Answer: A pen.

Harry Marsh (6)
St Oswald's CE Primary School, Ashbourne

Head In The Clouds

I am taller than a double-decker bus.
I can see what a bird can see but I'm not a
bird.
I am as graceful as a swan.
My tongue is black and long.
I have beautiful long legs but I can't dance.
My skin is like a jigsaw.
What am I?

Answer: A giraffe.

Nancy Lou Archer (6)
St Oswald's CE Primary School, Ashbourne

High Up In The Sky

I grow from a seed.
A part of me is hollow.
Squirrels run along me.
I have bark but I don't make a noise.
Birds sometimes build nests on me.
The bottom of me is underground.
Some of me stays green forever.
What am I?

Answer: A tree.

Ray Marsh (7)
St Oswald's CE Primary School, Ashbourne

In The Woodlands

I come out when you are in bed,
I have a tail that is bushy and red.
My babies are called cubs
And I belong to a family of dogs.
I live in a den,
My favourite dinner is the farmer's hen.
What am I?

Answer: A fox.

William Davies (6)
St Oswald's CE Primary School, Ashbourne

5ft 2

She kisses me and hugs me,
Bakes my favourite cakes,
Picks me up but is sometimes late.
She tucks me in at bedtime,
Cares for me when I'm ill,
And always has time for a story.
Who is she?

Answer: My mummy.

Sadie Burton (7)
St Oswald's CE Primary School, Ashbourne

Barking Bark

I have big, bushy hair.
If you count my rings,
You will know how old I am.
I have a strong stand.
I live in forests and grassy plains.
I am very useful.
I am a plant.
What am I?

Answer: A tree.

Lenny Lourie (7)
St Oswald's CE Primary School, Ashbourne

Noisy Place

Noisy place to be,
Lots of people in me.
Food in me,
I smell good.
I will hurt your ears,
There's lots going on.
I'm sometimes warm,
Sometimes cold.
What am I?

Answer: A kitchen.

Luciana Checketts (7)
St Oswald's CE Primary School, Ashbourne

The Whirl

I come in different colours.
I am long and windy.
I can live inside or outside.
I can be stripy, spotty or plain.
I am very useful.
I like being in gardens.
What am I?

Answer: A hosepipe.

Ottilie Godden (7)
St Oswald's CE Primary School, Ashbourne

Stable!

I have a long mane that you can brush.
I like to eat carrots and hay.
I have a loud neigh when I am scared.
I can run very, very fast.
I can be in a herd.
What am I?

Answer: A horse.

Zoe-Dee Barclay (7)
St Oswald's CE Primary School, Ashbourne

The New Arrival

I can be noisy,
I can be quiet.
I'm very small
But I grow to be very big.
I need a lot of help
And I love cuddles.
Who am I?

Answer: My baby sister, Dotty.

Poppy Clayton (7)
St Oswald's CE Primary School, Ashbourne

What Am I?

I have a green stem with a yellow middle.
I am sometimes fiddly with coloured petals
around the edge.
Sometimes I'm in a hedge.
What am I?

Answer: A flower.

Lily Butt (7)
St Oswald's CE Primary School, Ashbourne

Land Ahoy!

I live at sea
But I'm not a fish.
I love water
But I cannot drink.
Birds fly above me,
Fish swim below me.
What am I?

Answer: A ship.

Myles Edward Davies (7)
St Oswald's CE Primary School, Ashbourne

Heavy

I come in different makes.
I have a cab.
I have a bed.
I have four wheels.
I am known as a HGV.
What am I?

Answer: A lorry.

Taylor Hambleton-Harrison (6)

St Oswald's CE Primary School, Ashbourne

Something Missing In The Zoo

It is brown
It has sharp teeth
It eats salmon
It can live in the wild
What is it?

Answer: A bear.

Oliver Whitaker (6)

St Oswald's CE Primary School, Ashbourne

King Of The Sea

I have hooves but they don't clip-clop.
I bob along and don't stop.
I go *neigh* and I have a curly tail.
You might even see me if you go for a sail.
I live in the sea and you can't ride on me.
My daddy carries me when I'm a baby.
What am I?

Answer: A seahorse.

Cairistiona Smith (7)

Whaley Bridge Primary School, Whaley Bridge

Majestic

I am brown but can also be white, grey or black.
I can be wild or I can be tamed.
I am big and strong.
I can be fast and slow.
I wear shoes and you wear a hat.
I can take you wherever you want in a cart, carriage or on my back.
What am I?

Answer: A horse.

Kit Garside (5)

Whaley Bridge Primary School, Whaley Bridge

It Can Chop Stuff

It can chop stuff.
It can come in blue, red, purple and green.
It is in films.
If you have it, you are lucky.
You can be on the good side of it or the dark side.
If you're not careful, your arms can come off.
What is it?

Answer: A lightsaber.

Nate Cooper (7)
Whaley Bridge Primary School, Whaley Bridge

Colours

I am very colourful.
I match anything.
You can't see me.
I am normally scaly and green.
You will find me in the sandy desert.
What am I?

Answer: A chameleon.

Darcy Hodgson (6)
Whaley Bridge Primary School, Whaley Bridge

Ocean

I live in the ocean.
I squirt out water.
I have a hole in my back.
I am big and strong.
I have a tail.
I have a horn.
What am I?

Answer: A narwhal.

Nancy Caitlin Kerr (7)
Whaley Bridge Primary School, Whaley Bridge

Tall!

I am long.
I have a long neck.
I have spots.
I have yellow and brown spots.
I have four legs.
I have two horns.
What am I?

Answer: A giraffe.

Grace Vickers (6)
Whaley Bridge Primary School, Whaley Bridge

The Hero

He has a hammer.
He is big and strong.
His name is God of Thunder.
He lives on Asgard.
He is an Avenger.
Who is he?

Answer: Thor.

Sophie Ashworth (6)
Whaley Bridge Primary School, Whaley Bridge

Furry

I am furry and hairy.
I don't drink or eat or walk.
I have eyes but I can't see.
What am I?

Answer: A teddy bear.

Frankie Margaret Dorothy Yaya Knowles (7)

Whaley Bridge Primary School, Whaley Bridge

In The Life Of A...

I am black, white and orange.
I live in the woods.
I am nocturnal.
I eat chickens.
What am I?

Answer: A fox.

Hollie Jones (6)
Whaley Bridge Primary School, Whaley Bridge

Flying

I have a blue, red and yellow costume.
I have a hammer.
I am a hero.
Who am I?

Answer: Thor.

Sebastian Hilditch (7)
Whaley Bridge Primary School, Whaley Bridge

YoungWriters
Est.1991

YOUNG WRITERS
INFORMATION

We hope you have enjoyed reading this book – and that you will continue to in the coming years.

If you're a young writer who enjoys reading and creative writing, or the parent of an enthusiastic poet or story writer, do visit our website **www.youngwriters.co.uk**. Here you will find free competitions, workshops and games, as well as recommended reads, a poetry glossary and our blog.

If you would like to order further copies of this book, or any of our other titles, then please give us a call or visit **www.youngwriters.co.uk**.

Young Writers
Remus House
Coltsfoot Drive
Peterborough
PE2 9BF
(01733) 890066
info@youngwriters.co.uk